A CHAMPION'S
PATH

A CHAMPION'S
PATH

RACE TEAM TACTICS FOR BUSINESS

BE EXTRAORDINARY

DEREK DALY

ISBN: 978-1-937747-82-4
LCCN: 2016962815

Cover and Interior layout by Tom Heffron
Copyedit by Leah Noel
Proofread by Danielle Magnuson

On the cover
(top): Derek Daly, with his racing helmet on, ready for action.

(Bottom): Lewis Hamilton at Circuit of the Americas in Texas.
He is part of an extraordinary F1 team.

octanepress.com

DEDICATION

This book is dedicated to my mother, Nellie Daly. She demonstrates on a daily basis what unconditional love and support are.

CONTENTS

INTRODUCTION

How do we inspire a workforce to sustain high performances in dynamic, challenging, and competitive environments? Most big companies have access to funding, training, and technology yet still lack the ability to fully access human potential. The increased pace of business in today's world has brought a brand of turbulence that can cloud our direction.

This book will transport you through the high-speed developments used in auto racing, one of the most dynamic sports platforms in the world. The level of competition and funding found in Formula One and open-wheel racing has forced teams to develop some of the world's most advanced tactics for maximizing team performance. High-level professional open-wheel racing is a high-intensity sport, demanding exacting human performance in an environment of constant pressure and tight time frames. A sport that pushes people to the edges and boundaries of what might be possible. A sport that provides an ideal business model for today.

In 2001, bestselling author Jim Collins explained well how companies move from being good to being great in his book *Good to Great: Why Some Companies Make the Leap and Others Don't*. For many of the companies he highlights, at some point leadership felt being good was good enough. At one time, in the 1980s and much of the 1990s, being good was enough to be successful in sports and in business. But as technology began to change everything in the mid- to late 1990s, you had to move from good to great in sports and business to be successful. The dawn of the new century further accelerated that, and around 2010, because of ongoing technological advances and tightening regulations, being great even came under pressure. Great was even being questioned. It became evident to the great leaders that the great toolbox needed even more tools; great was no longer sufficient to be competitive. Winners had to then make the leap from great to *extraordinary*.

New technology flooded the market and our businesses had access to data at an unprecedented rate. Increased regulations greatly restricted our business and sports freedoms, and we were suddenly faced with a need to *out-think* the competition. We were forced to get faster and better. We were forced to think differently. We were forced to adopt a new culture. Not necessarily a culture of *success*, or a culture *of winning*, but a culture of *extraordinary*. Companies that transitioned from going faster to being faster also moved from being great to being extraordinary.

What if you and your team could progress beyond great? Motor racing at the highest levels provides real examples of such teams of people. In the early 2000s, the hammer of regulation change restricted the on-track development process of race cars. What once took place in public view was forced indoors to the simulation boardroom. The window to be competitive became narrower than ever. This led to a smaller number of teams being able to visit the victory podium to celebrate on a more regular basis. Those teams had to expand to unfamiliar reaches and had to become extraordinary to win. This book explores where extraordinary lives.

CHAPTER 1

A Formula for Success

My humble Irish beginnings in Dublin City, Ireland, provided an interesting backdrop to the fast-paced glamorous and dangerous world of Formula One. Having progressed from the dirt tracks to the ultimate performance platform, I learned that authentic and transparent principles provide true anchor platforms to build greatness. Formula One is a highly specialized industry that provides no place to hide. No place to pretend and certainly, as they say, no rest for the wicked.

Formula One: Exacting Human Performance

Formula One exposes all weaknesses. Sometimes the *strong* do not even survive. Unlike stick-and-ball sports, where one well-executed play can overcome a litany of mistakes, you seldom recover from a small mistake in Formula One. Small mistakes in Formula One can cost you any chance of on-track success—and can actually cost you your life. That parameter is what forced some Formula One teams to transition from great to extraordinary.

Derek's first dirt track championship-winning car in 1972.

DEREK DALY COLLECTION

Derek's Williams FW08 at the French Grand Prix in Dijon, 1982. DEREK DALY COLLECTION

Indianapolis 500: Faster Is Better

A very similar path was laid at the Indianapolis 500 in the 1980s, where good teams could win the largest attended single-day sports event in the world. When the speed of the race increased greatly in the 1990s, the need for much greater levels of detail and preparation dictated that only great teams won consistently. Nowadays, with the governing body's need to control speeds, much tighter regulations have restricted the development of cars, which has increased the need for more exacting human performance and deeper thinking to succeed. This dictated that only outstanding teams of people win on a consistent basis.

CHAPTER 2

The Culture of Extraordinary

Extraordinary teams have very deliberate disciplines that are fundamental to their success. These disciplines create the culture fabric that is then woven throughout the organization. Extraordinary teams willingly live between the turbulent edges of outstanding success and embarrassing failures. Their culture becomes the glue for the turbulence. They develop a sustained ability to be successful because of this deliberate culture. It's not just a culture of success—it's a culture of *extraordinary*.

The Advent of Extraordinary

You may have never thought of this before, but it is an amazing fact that in the National Football League (American football, for my international readers), on any given Sunday, 50 percent of the teams win.

In my business at the end of the day, the pressure by default is always greater because there is one winning team. Usually it's an extraordinary team, whose members are aligned with one another and who communicate effectively. They have a vision, they take intelligent risks, they create trust, and they use change as fuel. They have a plan and execute the plan under pressure on racetracks across the globe.

In an American football or soccer game, you can make a significant mistake and you will probably get a second chance. In motorsports, in general, there is no second chance after a significant mistake. In the National Football League (NFL), if a quarterback, through poor preparation, makes a mistake, he might lose a down. At the very worst, he might lose a game. Poor preparation and mistakes in my business, at 225 miles per hour, might cost a driver his life.

Motor racing, at the highest levels, is a sport that challenges people physically, mentally, intellectually, and emotionally. The speed, danger, rewards, and cost push team members to those outer edges and boundaries of what might be possible. What if we could learn to push ourselves to those outer edges on a daily basis? What if the outer edges could become our new normal? What if we could learn to go beyond our best? If we had the desire to move into an exceptional neighborhood, what road map might we use to get there?

What Is the Right Formula?

In 1982, the Williams Formula One team that I raced for spent $25 million running two cars in the world championship. Back then, people said that would never last. The perception was that there was no way Formula One would ever generate that amount of commercial sponsorship, year in and year out, to be able to spend and compete at that level. Today, to run at that level, the budget is $350 million, and remarkably, it has never been bigger.

Formula One today is one of the largest watched sports in the world. Major manufacturers use it as an image creation tool and a global exposure platform to make a statement—that their designers, engineers, technology, manufacturing ability, etc. can produce a product that can take on the world's best teams of people and products—and win. In Formula One, performance benchmarking is always relative to the competition.

In the early eighties in Formula One, the fastest average lap speeds were just over 150 miles per hour. People were suitably impressed. However, at the Indy 500 in 1977, the 200-miles-per-hour mark was broken in qualifying by Tom Sneva. People were again suitably impressed. A race car traveling at 200 miles per hour covers the length of a football field every second.

By the year 2010 at the Indy 500, you were not allowed to pass your rookie test if you could only do 200 miles per hour. Two hundred miles per hour was no longer considered fast enough to compete. You would be considered a hazard on the racetrack. In fact, you would be black flagged off the racetrack and sent home because of your inability to keep up with the competition—quite *extraordinary.*

CHAPTER 3

Victory Celebrations

During a twenty-five-year television broadcasting career, I traveled the world commentating on Formula One and Indycar races. At the end of those great races, the winning teams would enjoy the privilege of celebrating on the victory podium. The victory podium in motor racing can be regarded as a visual report card. The report card shows exactly how well you did as a team. The coveted trip to the podium is where the mechanics, engineers, and managers all go with their driver to celebrate their collective success. On that day, against the competition, no matter what the pressure was, no matter what immediate decisions had to be taken, they were the very best. The results of how they operated their business model on that day were transparent for all to see. The winning teams make a visual statement when celebrating on the victory podium that measures their risk-reward outcomes at *extraordinary* levels.

The largest single-day sports event (for attendance) in the world is the Indianapolis 500. During celebrations on the victory podium, the driver is presented with a bottle of milk—a

The victory podium is where teams go to make a statement: *We were the best today against all competition.* LAT

tradition that started in 1936 when winner Louis Meyer asked for a drink of buttermilk. The American Dairy Association has continued this now-iconic celebratory moment ever since.

In Formula One, the winning drivers spray champagne. This tradition started in 1967 with American Dan Gurney, who spontaneously sprayed champagne while celebrating after winning the 24 Hours of Le Mans with A. J. Foyt.

Without question, *extraordinary* cultures know the importance of celebrating their victories and *then* debriefing with honesty, trust, and humbleness to attain the same results the next time.

While conducting research during my broadcasting career, I was amazed that the number of teams that ever made it to the victory podium in Formula One or at the Indy 500 was so small. I asked a really simple question: *Why?*

Four-time Indy 500 champion Rick Mears holds the traditional bottle of milk on the victory podium. LAT

American driver Dan Gurney started the tradition of spraying champagne from the victory podium in 1967 after winning the 24 Hours of Le Mans race.

RAINER SCHLEGELMILCH

Why was the number so small? What was so special about these teams? What did they do that was a little different? Did they communicate differently? Did they plan differently? Did they execute differently? Did they have a vision that was unusual? What was it about these people? Were they better under pressure? Did they separate emotional decision making from intellectual decision making at a higher level? I wanted to know the answers and I had access to the biggest stars in our sport, such as Mario Andretti, Roger Penske, A. J. Foyt, Danny Sullivan, and Michael Schumacher, and the great teams such as Ferrari, Mercedes, and McLaren. I didn't know it at the time, but the answers would provide the foundation for how extraordinary teams of people behaved.

The answers were fascinating and they allowed me to see completely under the skin of my sport and to understand more clearly why only a small number of teams were successful—a small number of extraordinary teams. Teams who had a deliberate behavior—an unusual culture . . . *a culture of extraordinary*. I finally had the address of where extraordinary lived.

CHAPTER 4

....

Trust

When I competed for the first time at the Indianapolis 500 in 1983, the fastest drivers could lap at an average speed of 200 miles per hour. They would drive for 2 ½ miles down long straights and through four 90-degree corners every forty-five seconds. Tom Sneva officially broke through the 200-mile-per-hour barrier for the first time in history in 1997. Six years later, I could do an average lap speed of about 199 miles per hour, but I could never break through that magical barrier of 200 miles per hour.

I was told that as a European road racer, I didn't understand the correct driving technique for a high-speed oval. People recommended that I walk down the pit lane to a veteran and ask him to explain the required technique. My target was a good friend of mine, a true legend of our sport, Mario Andretti. Mario was a Formula One world champion and also won the Indy 500, so he had been through all of this before.

My question was not really unusual. Rookies usually needed help from veterans at superspeedways.

Derek and his trusted friend Mario Andretti share a laugh many years after Mario gave Derek advice on how to break through the 200-mile-per-hour barrier at Indy.
DEREK DALY COLLECTION

I listened intently for words of wisdom that I might be unfamiliar with. He said the required technique was actually very simple. When you are racing down the long front straight, he said tell your brain to tell your foot not to get off the gas pedal until after you've turned the steering wheel into the corner.

My first connection to his recommendation was virtual. I could visualize what was needed first. I could see it in my mind. It might have sounded easy, but it was definitely a mindset change for me.

I zipped up my fireproof suit, tightened my helmet strap, and got wedged into my car. As the seat belts were squeezed down, I could feel my heartbeat rise. There is a natural tension when a driver is strapped into a 200-mile-per-hour projectile when he is expected to flirt with its explosive performance capabilities, within an artificially walled environment.

As I fired up the 850-horsepower turbocharged engine and left my pit, Mario's words of advice were in clear focus. An Indy car accelerates past 100 miles per hour in less than three seconds. My straight-line speed down the long front straight was about 212 miles per hour. The key to a high average lap speed is not to lose too much speed going through the corners. As usual, everything seemed noisy as the turbulent wind was whistling by.

As the first corner drew closer, I remembered exactly what he said. Things happen really fast at 212 miles per hour, but the closer to the corner I got, I began to think maybe I was not brave enough to do this. My foot was planted on the gas pedal. The car was still picking up speed and I was still questioning whether I was brave enough to do it. Right about the point of no return and with Mario's words ringing in my head, a doubting thought suddenly flashed through my mind:

Do you think he told me the truth?

It's always funny when I tell people this story, but it didn't seem that funny at the time from inside the cockpit. Of course the buried question was: Was it safe for me to disengage emotionally from what I had believed to be true?

I backed off the power, slowed down quite a bit, caught my breath, and drove through the corner as I had in the past. I would have to try again.

Next time I forced myself to be a little braver. I went a little deeper into the corner, but I still didn't feel brave enough, so I backed off again. The third attempt was better. I found it difficult to do what Mario said, but at least I was going to trust his advice and push it to my personal limit. I took a deep breath, grabbed the steering wheel tightly, tightened every muscle in my body, and entered Turn One with my foot flat on the power. I could feel my whole body tighten with tension as I drove deeper into the unknown. My hands tightened their grip on the steering wheel even more as I actually got to the point of no return. My corner entry speed was higher that I'd ever experienced before.

The pressure began to build in the steering wheel as the g-force loads increased, signifying that I now had the car in high-stress mode as I entered the corner. I didn't lift off the power until after I'd turned the steering wheel into the corner—just like he told me. When I did back off as the corner tightened up, the car settled into a nice groove of grip and I felt safe. My body's tension began to release into a more relaxed state. My entry speed was faster than I had ever gone before—over 212 miles per hour before I eased off the power a little. The car was good enough to stick to the road and I had just proven that I was brave enough to push to that limit.

I used the same new technique at the end of the long back straight into Turn Three, and when I flashed by the start-finish line, my speed was officially recorded at 201 miles per hour. I was thrilled. I had broken through the barrier by learning a new technique. Believe it or not, I never did another lap speed below 200 miles per hour the rest of the practice session.

Of course, I thought Mario shared his information to help me—and then I realized he didn't. He shared his information and experience to help him, and everybody else who might be on the racetrack in close proximity to me (a rookie) and at such high speeds. Can you imagine a rookie, who did not know the key technique, at 212 miles per hour in an open-wheel racecar making unusual or unpredictable moves? It could be catastrophic.

I am about to share with you an astounding secret. At the speed that I was going, I trusted my life to Mario and his information. And I wouldn't hesitate to send young drivers for his counsel today, because I know I can trust him implicitly. And then I had the big moment of realization. I realized that *trust* is the very foundation of the extraordinary teams of people who get to the victory podium on a more regular basis. Trust is never built faster than by willingly sharing what you know with the people around you to make them better. I like to call it *tandem trust*. The power of sharing is when your knowledge and information is shared with the people around you to help them, and how it then actually helps you too. The result of tandem trust is that the team around you gets stronger with an admirable, solid trust-based foundation.

CHAPTER 5

Where Does Extraordinary Live?

Extraordinary people and teams understand the power of sharing information to lift up the entire foundation of their craft.

If our thoughts create our emotions, and our emotions create our behavior, it stands to reason that to change our behavior, we would need to change our thoughts. This is known as a renewing of the mind. If we were to define what extraordinary looks like, it might be a select group of people who think a little differently—and therefore act a little differently and therefore succeed more often.

If we peel back the curtain on my sport, we can see some of the specifics of what extraordinary looks like, both on and off the racetrack. We can get a feel for how the extraordinary teams think and operate. The most successful American team owner in our sport, Roger Penske, said that he does not necessarily put people in a position to be the very best they can be. Rather he

The great Ferrari team is driven by the fear of
being beaten. LAT

likes to put people in a position where they *want* to be the very
best they can be. *Wanting* it is a different mindset. Wanting
opens the door to a unique culture—a *culture of extraordinary*.
So what makes the culture of extraordinary team members a
little different? Let's examine some of those who fought to
establish this culture of extraordinary.

During his tenure of presiding over some of Ferrari's greatest
days in Formula One, former team manager Jean Todt said great
teams like Ferrari worked hard because they believed they could
be beaten at any moment. The team was almost unbeatable,
though, and had an unbelievable run of success under Todt.

Their refusal to believe they couldn't be beaten was how they
lived and breathed. It allowed them to access the part of their

"They live convinced they could be beaten tomorrow."

—*Jean Todt, CEO, Ferrari*

being that drove them forward and upward at the same time. It's not a pressure to think and live this way, but more of an adventure and a desire. If you think you could be beaten tomorrow, and you are a naturally competitive person who wants to win, you will do anything to put yourself into a position of advantage. If you are not a naturally competitive person within one of these teams, success-oriented team members will surround you. This competitive spirit can lift your commitment because you will not want to be the weak link.

Performance gains can be found living and acting on the outer edges of what might be possible. They nudge up against the edge to maintain a pressure to keep moving the boundary a little farther out. It's a controlled edge where risk and risk management intersect as a complement. They thrive out on the margins and boundaries. They find it adventurous and look forward to the challenge. They know that there will be financial, as well as emotional, rewards for success. Operating on the outer borders can put people by default into a risk-taking mode. These teams, however, take what is known as intelligent risks. They take pride in demonstrating what it's like to operate out on the edges as only the extraordinary can.

Financial and emotional rewards can be intoxicating. We become most vulnerable in times of success. Success sometimes causes us to take our foot off the accelerator. When exceptional teams win, they immediately start plotting how to do it again. When they lose, and they sometimes do, the driver does not blame everyone else for the lack of performance. Working harder is a given, but working smarter next time is more prevalent within these teams. They contain any celebrations to critical (but reasonable levels) and subdue relaxation after

"They live with, and understand, that significant performance gains happen at the edges and boundaries of people and equipment."

—*Derek Daly*

success. Trophies fuel hunger and a starvation for more. Today's success is boxed and shipped while the next race plan is being finalized. Overconfidence and invincibility become their enemy. They are masters of the chase and the hunt never ends. Their life's discipline is rooted in high performance and they feel privileged to be placed in a high-performance spotlight.

"They live in constant disbelief of the sustainability of their own performance."

—*Derek Daly*

CHAPTER 6

Preparation: Time and Attitude Invested Are Key

Now that we have looked into the psyche of the extraordinary, let's look at some of the hard skills associated with these successful teams. The first one may seem a little basic: **preparation**. When you have racing drivers who literally trust their lives to the people who work on the cars, as you can imagine, world-class preparation is HUGE in my business.

Preparation does not happen by accident. Those who become *extraordinary* at the world-class level insist on having sufficient time for it, and it pays off. Perfecting a skill that increases your odds of showing up on the victory podium more often does not happen by accident. If your attitude isn't aligned and consistent, get out of the way. No team can ever prepare to become extraordinary with inconsistent variables.

Proof of Concept: The Indy 500 Starting Grid

In racing, when you participate in a qualifying session to decide the starting grid order, the fastest cars and teams start at the front. Do you think it's a coincidence that when I do my television interviews on the front of the grid at the Indy 500, I inevitably see the best painted, best sponsored, best *prepared* cars right up at the front of the grid? The mechanics are usually immaculately dressed. They are proudly and confidently standing by their car and driver, ready to take on the competition. All the job lists are taken care of and they are ready to execute on their plan. They are not competing internally against their teammates but collectively against their outside competitors. These teams were preparing early enough to have time to refine their aesthetics.

Front-of-the-grid cars are usually better prepared to take on the competition. DEREK DALY COLLECTION

Middle-of-the-grid teams are already well behind
the faster cars. DEREK DALY COLLECTION

This is a signal of extraordinary. It makes it so much
easier for sponsors/partners to envision the value of sharing
this space.

When I move to the middle of the grid to do my interviews,
I'll see some pretty good teams there and they are glad to be in
the Indy 500, but these teams are already looking forward at
teams of people who have already demonstrated they've done
a better job—and the race hasn't even started yet.

Now do you think it's a coincidence that when I move to the
back of the grid I no longer see as many immaculately dressed
mechanics, nor do I see as much sponsorship support for these
back-of-the-grid cars? If you look at the image on the next page
of a back-of-the-grid team, there's a mechanic on his hands and
knees, he has tools in his hands, and he's actually working on
the gearbox on the starting grid of the largest attended single-
day sporting event in the world.

Failure at the Indy 500 usually starts from the back of the grid. DEREK DALY COLLECTION

Now do you think it's a coincidence that the fall-out and failure rate at the Indy 500 also starts from the back of the grid? Because it is directly proportional to the amount of preparation the back-of-the-grid teams put in, before they go against the competition. And the back of the grid is inevitably populated by teams of people who probably have the resources available to them, but just didn't bother to use them. Some might even play the blame game for being in this location.

They may resent that things have changed so fast and just wish it could be easier to be competitive—like it was in years past. But there's a double whammy for the teams that are on the back of the grid. First, you have taken yourself out of the position of advantage. And the double whammy is you might have given that position of advantage to your competition.

Let me ask you a question:

**With regard to your preparation for
what you do every day, where do
you think you are on the starting
grid for the race you are in currently?**

Everybody I ask that question to will know their own personal answer. And if you clearly see yourself up at the front of the grid, you are beginning to emulate those excellent teams that get on the victory podium more often. If at any time you, or the people who are in your sphere of influence, are not clearly at the front of the grid, the resources are probably available to get there. The winners are not busy resenting each other. They are maximizing the resources they do have by helping each other and focusing on the success of the organization. They use refinement to their extraordinary advantage!

So just ask yourself this question every morning:

**Where am I on the starting grid today,
with regard to my preparation for
the race I'm in every day?**

My hope is you are already embracing the *culture of extraordinary,* and clearly see yourself right up at the front of the grid.

CHAPTER 7

Innovation and Creativity: The Rich Vein That Fuels Success

Innovation both violates and creates tradition. Modern tradition just happens faster and does not last as long. In a world where software is supplanting the need to think, the lifeblood of future success is still the ever-curious human mind.

Automotive research and development was born in America and spread globally. Research and development is the cornerstone of the car manufacturing business globally. Non-linear thinking is crucial in my sport and it's expressed within the extraordinary teams by the ability to be innovative and creative. But make no mistake about it: They do not expect research and development to be the exclusive place for re-evaluation.

In 1911, the winning car in the first Indianapolis 500 had the very first rear-view mirror ever on a vehicle. In the initial race, it was commonplace to have a ride-along mechanic doing what our mirrors now accomplish. He'd look and see who was behind the driver and alert him if need be. If anything broke on the car, he might be able to fix it. However, carrying this additional lump of human ballast around for 500 miles would obviously slow the car down. The *Marmon Wasp* team took a risk. They believed their car to be so well-prepared that it would not break down, so they threw out the riding mechanics.

To see what was happening behind the driver, they devised a little piece of mirrored glass above the cockpit. Suddenly, the rear-view mirror was born. Very soon, rear-view mirrors appeared on every road car. To emphasize how

The very first rear-view mirror, developed to help the *Marmon Wasp* team avoid having the weight of a ride-along mechanic. DEREK DALY COLLECTION

flexible extraordinary teams need to be, it is not likely that in 1911 there was a formalized research and development department.

In 1949 Volvo put seat belts in the car for the first time; however, racing developed the stretch nylon that better absorbed energy when a driver hit something really hard. Lightweight, energy-absorbing crash helmets were developed first in competition. Bulletproof visors became necessary because if a stone was kicked up at 200 miles per hour, it was traveling at the speed of a bullet. Radial tires, fuel injection, and even the fire-resistant clothing now used in children's pajamas were developed because of race drivers' fireproof suits. Nothing develops faster than in the environment of healthy competition.

Unless teams are sprinkled with creative thinkers who are encouraged to find a better way, the threat to becoming irrelevant looms large. This creative thinking does not happen unless actively encouraged. If brilliant software has replaced our need to think creatively today, then do something *extraordinary*. Put the wild idea box visible for all to see.

CHAPTER 8

How Does Extraordinary Behave?

W e all agree that there is a deliberate behavior within extraordinary teams that keeps increasing their odds of success.

The Mercedes Formula One team is extraordinary in every sense. DEREK DALY COLLECTION

"Successful teams are full of individualist thinkers, who transition to team players for their actions."

—Derek Daly

Extraordinary team members, with their rich veins of curiosity, are constantly challenged to be individualistic thinkers. These are the people with the wild ideas who are forever stretching for what might be possible. Extraordinary teams place themselves mentally in the driver's seat. They know that success is no longer just about a better product; it's about every facet of the business. These individuals become invaluable because they become the internal beacons who stretch the organization by example. Not only are they concerned with the health of their organization, but they keep a discerning eye on the competition.

However, taking personal credit does not drive them. Does this describe you?

"Extraordinary teams encourage innovation to create new sources of high performance, to stretch and grow both the efficiency and effectiveness of their process."

—Derek Daly

In an effort to control budgets, regulations have been tightened down in our sport. The past freedoms to run teams and build cars have been replaced by restrictive rules that challenge the way we think and operate.

Seldom in our sport are we in a position to have a product that is head and shoulders above the competition. Successful businesses of the future are predicated on their process of efficiency. That's what will make them effective. This is when ordinary becomes the enemy. When sanctioning bodies tightened up the regulations for race car builders, it was no longer possible to simply out-spend the competition and build a faster race car. The winning teams then had to out-think the competition in addition to out-racing them. Innovation has always been the anchor of success in motorsports, but extraordinary teams were required to add innovative thinking to the process of how they executed their race plans.

"Success requires a range of leaders, committed individuals throughout the team who are willing to accept responsibility of leadership, regardless of their formal authority."

—Derek Daly

Extraordinary team members don't have to be told, "you're a leader"—it's expected. It's ingrained in them; it's hardwired in them. It's part of the fabric within extraordinary teams. Outstanding leadership also steps out of the way to let more than just one person shine. No driver, regardless of how extraordinary, has ever crossed the finish line without the car. So regardless of the formal authority, there's a portfolio of extraordinary leaders who permeate throughout these teams—individuals who want to show and prove that they are invaluable. They consider it a privilege to be challenged to step up. These individuals uncover newer, better, more efficient ways to remove the speed bumps that are slowing them down. These team members certainly do not add speed bumps by failing to help each other or wasting time overreacting when leadership is growing.

CHAPTER 9

Choosing to Be Extraordinary

Choice is one of the most powerful words in the English language. The greatest power we all possess is the power to choose. Choose whether we want to survive or succeed. Choose whether we want to be like everybody else or be *extraordinary*. When you strive for excellence, anything can happen.

If you choose to be extraordinary, your future is in your hands and those hands will have more power than the ordinary.

If you want to act differently, you have to think differently. If you want to create an extraordinary culture, you have to think like a *culture of extraordinary*. That means you have to activate some specific choices. Choose whether you want to add to your existing giftedness. Choose whether anything you read in this book resonates beyond the page and can be further embraced in your everyday life. Choose whether your skills can be enhanced and used to radiate to others.

"A better you makes a better us."

—Derek Daly

If you make that choice to become better than you ever were before, some amazing things can happen. If you add to your abilities, my promise to you is that *a better you makes a better us*. And remember, you must be emotionally open and available to engage in order to do this. An aligned and better *us* provides the structure and foundation for an extraordinary team that can find its members celebrating on the victory podium on a more regular basis.

If you are personally equipped with more tools than ever before, it may not matter what the competition does in the future, because you will be equipped for whatever comes your way in the next decade.

We are all in a race every day. If you want to win, you have to have the right tools and equipment. Then you need the right people using the tools and equipment. When you venture out of the pit lane onto the racetrack, your challenge will be to push down on the accelerator pedal a little harder. As the speed picks up, you might need to put it in a higher gear. Allow yourself to take intelligent risks and only glance in the rear-view mirror, as you safely speed toward success.

Remember, you will not decide your future. You will decide your habits. Your habits will then decide your future. When those habits direct you toward the victory podium, you are ready to *GO out and BE extraordinary!*

ACKNOWLEDGMENTS

My deepest thanks go to two people who really helped shape what this book would become. They are . . .

Michelle Sybesma, Professional Skills Consulting. I leaned on Michelle's considerable expertise to expand upon the powerful business connection to the motorsports world. She is largely responsible for the concept of *Be Extraordinary.*

Richard West. Richard and I roamed many of the same Formula One paddocks across the world for many years. I drew great inspiration from his knowledge and experience that is captured admirably in his book, *Performance at the Limit*, now in its fourth edition.

INDEX